Dangerous Enough

Also by Alison Stone

They Sing at Midnight
From the Fool to the World

Dangerous Enough

poems by

Alison Stone

PRESA PRESS
ROCKFORD, MI

Acknowledgments

Poems in this book have appeared in the following publications: *1st of the Month, 5 AM, Ark, Boomer Girls: Poems by Women from the Baby Boom Generation* (Pamela Gemin & Paula Sergi, Editors; University Of Iowa Press;1999), *Cider Press Review, First of the Year: 2008* (Vol. I; Benj DeMott, Editor; Transaction Publishers; 2008), *First of the Year: 2009* (Vol. II; Benj DeMott, Editor; Transaction Publishers; 2010), *Forge, Great River Review, The Illinois Review, Many Mountains Moving, New York Quarterly, The Paris Review, Poetry, Slipstream, Snowy Egret, Sweet Nothings: An Anthology of Rock 'N Roll in American Poetry* (Jim Elledge, Editor; Indiana University Press; 1994), *Witness* and *Women Write Resistance* (Laura Madeline Wiseman, Ph.D., Editor; Hyacinth Girl Press; 2013)
Front cover art by Scott Baisden.
Back cover photo of author courtesy of Michael Stone.

For support and suggestions during the revision process, thanks to Kathi Aguero, Steve Huff, Dzvinia Orlowsky, Laure-Anne Bosselaar, Thom Ward, and the Peer Workshop women. Thanks to Roseanne Ritzema for believing in the book. Thanks to my family for time and understanding.

First Edition

Printed in the United States of America

ISBN: 978-0-9888279-3-6

Library of Congress Control Number: 2014930787

PRESA PRESS
PO Box 792   Rockford, Michigan 49341
presapress@aol.com   www.presapress.com

Dangerous Enough

to Michael

Contents

III.

I.

Mother, HIV+

Her husband crept from bed
to dance with men in bars or under
oak trees in the park.
He left her for
a trucker. Now he's dead.

He left her
with the bills, the kids,
the stink of chicken
fried the way he likes.
Her left hand's cold O.

Her son hugs
a Power Ranger.
Mommy, please don't
sleep so much.
Fevers burn
her curves away –
Bones fill with sand.

Almost Thirteen

1.
She can divide without paper, decline
Latin nouns. She wants to slow dance
at parties and learn to kiss with her tongue.

She hides her intellect
and fat thighs, love
for corny movies,

her deep voice, her tears.
Pale and unobjectionable,
she gets asked out by a gap-toothed boy

who shows her butterflies
propped on a shelf,
pins through their wings.

2.
Sleep evades her.
Dizzy from circular resentments,
she reads about

dead generals,
distracting herself
with someone else's war.

The dead can't
change their minds.
They can't forgive.

The dead
lie in cold beds –
disintegrate like books.

3.
Bright spider on a silver web, a field
of ordinary grass and bees, a grove of trees
who wear their souls as bark.

Birds dive into the deep lake of the sky.
As she sits, a tortoise, shell smooth as a table,
lumbers over the weeds. Disturbed

by her, the tortoise halts, pulls out its neck, and stares
with the face of a thick snake.
She stares back

satisfied to be a girl
meeting a tortoise
in a sun-streaked field.

Bat Mitzvah Lessons
with the Cantor

Nothing the rabbi says is true.
A twelve-year-old girl is a half-written book.
I belong to you.

My haftora is about leprosy, dead or oozing skin,
how touch can ruin a person.
Then she must wear a bell and chant, *unclean, unclean.*

You choose me for my awkwardness
in my new body, choose me
over the popular ones with sharp,

expensive clothes and loud laughter, choose me
for my breasts and my silence.
Mighty in black robes,

you chant each line,
commanding me to copy,
broad hands on my abdomen

to guide my breath. When you lock
your office door, I shut my eyes,
pretend to be rock.

I wobble in heels to the bimah.
The sanctuary's filled, my parents
beam from the front row. You hover

behind me as my voice shakes
and I lose my place in the prayers.
The rabbi says

I'm done with childhood,
a woman,
lovely in the eyes of God.

Hair to Sky

Fifteen years ago I jumped
into a fountain on a cute punk's dare.

Men with briefcases stared
as I wrung out my skirt on the train.

I was on my way
to everywhere, my body fluent

in the dialect of nightclubs,
all imperatives and exclamation points.

My hips were water whose
tides pulled men down.

Turquoise dye transformed
my hair to sky.

Now life's an apartment with scratched
tables and a fraying couch; lack

of sex the dull green wallpaper
that casts its pallor over everything.

I dig up the Clash and blare
them until neighbors

pound. Hair slicked,
lips black, I rifle

my trunk for a spiked belt
but remember Yogi Berra:

*If you can't copy him
don't imitate him.*

Rocks on Stone

When did we start swimming lessons?
What was the gerbil's name?
Above the graves, stale blue
October sky, your silence
punctuated by the chatter of birds.

Where should I seat
the drunk uncle? Rosemary
or cumin for the soup? Holidays
without you rough as rocks
left on your headstone, flecks
of mica sparkling with useless light.

After the Fall

Lawyers think my grief can turn to money.
They think this will make me smile,
my new smile, one side of my face
dumb as putty. Doctors tell me
I am lucky.
All the things I can still do!

My limbs grow unfamiliar.
Deep grooves of my muscles,
proof of heavy objects
hoisted, pre-dawn runs
through injury and rain, are blurring
like a charcoal sketch. Each day
more of me erases.

Religion fails
to make me see my body
as a useful but unnecessary car.
Wrapped in rough sheets
I feign sleep when the nurses
come with chipper questions
or a yellow lump of pudding on a tray.

Not on the List

A shrub flames
with God's word. Wrecked car
dangles from a cliff
until help comes.
Tumors vanish like smoke. A lover
wakes from a coma and asks
for coffee with milk.

Our deepest prayers answered
No,
the rest of us get
diapers, morphine, feeding tubes,
daily losses and indignities, implacable
as the sulky lump of an aide
who plunks herself in our best chair, reads
the Bible, and won't bathe my mother
because that isn't on her list.

Practicing

Friends with children
          ask if we are trying yet,
                    show photos of deliveries, bare butts

on bearskin rugs. I lie, *Just practicing.*
          My old eggs
                    may not make it.

This year, most phone calls bring
          a funeral or
                    worse. Even our cat has cancer.

My blood is a monthly disappointment.

Buddha said that suffering
          is caused by grasping
                    what we love. The cure is letting go,

so I try waving good-bye to our child, giving
          back her prom night, his first snow
                    fall. Holding nothing. Practicing.

Water Babies

1.
Judy Bloch and I play water babies for hours, stretching
the balloons' mouths around the hose, filling them
full enough to have heft but not so big
they burst. Sometimes we draw magic marker eyes with long
lashes, smiling cupid mouths. Mostly their bald
faces stare from doll strollers
we wheel around the yard, stopping
to cradle them and pat their jiggly backs.

We stay outside
as long as possible, far from her immaculate, cold house,
my brother's explosions. When we tire of mothering,
we play catch until the inevitable splat.

2.
Judy has a dog named Snow
who lets us tie a bonnet on him, push
a milk-filled bottle in his mouth.

Her parents have him
"put to sleep" for peeing on the rug.
She keeps his collar
in her treasure box.

3.
Floating, face relaxed, Lena labors
in her bathtub while dolphin
calls play in the background
and her husband croons.
I've only seen women
clenched and screaming,
on their backs in TV hospitals

surrounded by doctors
and machines.

Lena smiles, her eyes roll back,
and four loud breaths later,
her son slips into the water like a fish. She places
my fingers on the pulsing
cord. The air thick, charged – something
in the room with us, unnamable.

4.
My daughter refuses
to turn. Nineteen hours her spine
grinds into my tailbone
while I vomit and moan
from water tank to
shower to floor, the midwife
making me climb stairs,

the doula finally admitting
she doesn't actually
know acupressure.

5.
Forty-five, my body bleeds
heavily and often, loosens
its ties to the moon.

Ovaries fire,
pumping out
the last good eggs.

6.
Bunny Foo Foo dominates
our stereo, along with Mary Poppins
and the Muffin Man. My girl
turns David Bowie down. *You*

like such dumb music, Mommy.
Walking to school, she sings
under her breath about a lion
lulled to sleep in rustling
grass. She sees her friends and
drops my hand.

Sex Talk Among Women

On the way back from the Hamptons
we argue about language and sex,

how speech reduces women to the status
of a wall plate waiting for a plug.

Nail, screw, drive, thrust, penetrate, and *pork.*
We build our lives with words

and yet have never heard or read *engulf,
surround, enfold.*

We who last night bared
our bodies in the whirlpool are now divided

by the description of a penis.
You put the cover on *the mayonnaise jar;*

you don't put the jar in *the cover.*
         Yeah, but you put the jar in *the refrigerator.*

A refrigerator is a big, dumb, cold thing.
         Don't be angry – that's so Seventies.

A circle of women, we sat in steam
celebrating beauty and differences,

the sizes of our breasts, the flatness
or curve of bellies, the shades

of our pubic hair.
Voices rise and sharpen.

We miss our exit bickering,
ask directions at a deli

selling *Let Christ Help You Beat Temptation*
bumper stickers, day-glo condoms, cans of worms.

Palliative Care

Now that you are losing your body,
its specifics flood me – the bump

where your nose was broken,
your crooked prison peace-sign tattoo,

your hand on my
back as we kissed

near a pack of street toughs and the leader
yelled, *Some guys have all the luck.*

Eyes averted skyward, wooden
Jesus bleeds above a TV blaring,

*Beauty Queens and Drag Queens,
Who is Who?*

He knows you're with him, a nun
whispers. *Hearing is the last to go.*

Refusing to name your death, your relatives
will write *after a short illness;*

but the virus they admit to,
CMV, gives everything away

like an Adam's apple
above a mink stole.

The husky-voiced TV host tries
to temp us with his future

guests. You will die before *Bigamists Who Aren't Mormons.*

Your sister gasps
as a sequined diva rips off his wig.

The slick announcer promises
all secrets will be revealed.

Home Schooling

A phalanx of pencils, points bared,
new pens
oozing blue. Add in mother's
hunger, father's bible,
brother's fists. Subtract the female body.

Multiply by closets, fingernails
gnawed to blood.
Learn how loyalty
divides a child
from herself.
Lunch is cold baloney slapped

on Wonder Bread, insubstantial
as clenched teeth
which loosen, fall out. Then a fairy
brings coins with
a dead man's face.

A wrong sum
can be easily erased. The child
sings the songs she's taught,
pledges allegiance
covering her heart.

Back in My Teenage Bedroom

From Elvis to the Velvet Underground
they pose and sneer – Lux Interior
with the mic down his pants taped
next to feathered Joplin roosting

on Sid's spiky hair. Wendy O explodes
a bus, Hendrix burns and flames
shoot up toward Patti Smith's armpit,
Joey Ramone's extended hand.

Dull from years of low-heeled shoes
and tepid climaxes, I lie back
to face my first loves and remember
building this wall, hour after hour,

star upon star, sacrificing
lesser images on the back, scissors
digging grooves into my
middle finger and thumb.

Although their skins remain
unlined, some of them
have faded and bulge
in the middle. I drag myself up

and smooth them down. When they
watched over my bed, rough rhythms
filled me. Invincible, electric,
I nailed each guitar riff in the air.

Assimilation

*People who speak Spanish all have
outside jobs,* my daughter announces
as the Mow 'n Blow crew descend from a truck
to tame our lawn. I read her
a book about dark children dancing,
playing drums with wrinkled elders, eating
fried plantains. Bored, she grabs Dr. Seuss.
*I'm not Latin, Mommy,
I'm light pink like you.*

If your family would call, I tell my husband, *or if you made
rice and beans.*
            *Well if you stopped putting so much sunblock on her.
Maybe if we got somebody white to cut the grass.*

            I'm not that *dark.* He frowns when she
uses the brown crayon to shade him
flanked by purple flowers underneath a turquoise
stripe of sky. She hesitates before her own face
and then leaves it blank.

The Taste for Bad Boys
Starts Early

My daughter wants to marry Finn.
He's funny. He's older.

He's five. He dunked doll
clothes in the guppy tank, pushed

play-doh up his nose.
He calls her *poopyhead*.

She kisses the messy rainbow
Finn painted for her, jagged

arcs of orange, red, blue, black.
He's teaching her to jump off chairs.

I see her leap forward
thirteen years, come down crying

for a wise guy wannabe with powders in his pocket,
lies and other women on his tongue.

Maybe he slapped her,
robbed a Laundromat, gave

her the clap.
Maybe she's pregnant.

Mommy, watch!
She jumps again,

off-balance, out of breath
lands teetering

between the window
and the breakfast nook.

II.

Amtrak 137

I hope I'm dangerous enough. Bad
breath, bitten cuticles, the wad of shredded
tissue I blow into,
                              anything
to make this loud, round, sweaty
                              stranger shrink
to his side of the seat.

He keeps talking, and I nod –
                              why can't I
                              not nod? Pallid trees we pass
flop in the wind like fish.
There is nowhere else to go;
the bathroom's locked, the buffet
full of children.

As factories give way to cows we rattle
to a stop. The man touches my arm
and I zip my coat.
                              Close my eyes,
                              wait for
the train to start.

Dancing

This is our new dance, my mother calls out,
suddenly unable to walk, as my father
half drags, half carries her down the hall.

Once she dressed for dancing in big
earrings, clingy gowns. I watched her twist
her thick hair, then paint

her suddenly mysterious face.
My father watched the clock.
Fumbling with buttons, she tried

to sooth him. *Soon, I promise. Soon.*
He grumped out to wait
in the car. I helped her raise

her zipper, clasp a strand
of pearls. Her hands
shook when he honked the horn.

Days of couch to bathroom, chair to bed,
the living room and back. Despite bursitis
he maneuvers her, my mother wrapped

in a bathrobe, scarves and wig discarded,
apologizing, *This is too much for you.*
Step, pause, shuffle, shift of weight,

step, step, turn, my father
watching her, his movements slow and tender
as though they had all the time in the world.

Dirt

My husband, we are the cutting
that failed, the limp philodendron.

No honest violence
like a garden overturned. We are wrapped

in mealy bugs' cotton,
the cushion that chokes.

Masses of stems press the glass;
the spider plant weeps

frail white stars. At each touch,
leaves crumble. The sun doubles itself

in my knife's blade.
Tenderly, I cut away what is dead.

New York After

History holds us
like tight shoes, molding us
until what is twisted
feels normal. Even the bright
silly book I buy you ends
with beetles battling, a fox
trapped in a jar.
My husband says,

to babies words are merely
sibilants and glottals, music
like the restaurant ad I amused
you with yesterday – aloo
gobi, chana sag.
Mother, Muslim, burning, hope.

The Devil's in the Details

and marriage is a mess of them –
toilets, in-laws, dishes, sex.

Dizzy with kisses, duped
by the sly moon, I didn't notice

his endless preferences,
his moodiness which splatters

me like muddy water
shaken from a long-haired dog.

Not some big explosion – table
overturned, knives hurled at the wall –

but tiny daily disappointments
smoldering until the drapes ignite,

kitchen table kindling, our bedroom
a field of ash.

Rocket to Russia

We split the night
between the Rat and Spit, crash
at Ann's when the nightclubs close. Ashes
in the fish tank, plates
and panties in the sink.
I think Johnny wants me
'cause he dances with a hand
between my legs, but when I lie
on the bed he ignores me to boil
powder in a bottle cap, then nod
on a bench. Kat passes out
Ding-Dongs stolen from the deli
and laughs about the time she threw up
on a trick and had to pretend
she'd been poisoned.
I wake up with purple hair and Paul
beside me, grinning
as he tries to dye Jenni's bangs
blue. She rolls and stains
the pillowcase. Contact lenses feel
like glass, mouth tastes of socks.
Walking to the subway in cold
rain, I curse my mom
for lending me her pointy boots.
Jenni and I discuss Shakespeare
and mescaline, and why
our boyfriends prefer men.
A passing woman asks if I've been
mugged. Krazy Kolor has bled
down my forehead
and looks like a wound.
No time to answer her, I have to
get to school. We are
doing one of the important wars.

Letters Home from London

change me to a brand new person.
I'm losing that aggressive New York walk
we hope discourages muggers,

maniacs, and Bible thumpers.
Every man has cheekbones
and a band. Even the royal family

is amusing – effete Charles' raunchy letters to
his mistress, the Queen's frumpy, feathered hats.
Beneath my window, a photographer

puts droopy parrots on
tourists' shoulders, yanking them off again
if the tourists won't pay.

I struggle to avoid
the kitchen. Never at home would I be
so loose with the dishes. Roosting

in the sink, they advertise
a week of dinners like a menu.
After midnight, the Marquee

throbs, making me invincible
until a goth whose man I danced with
stabs me with her hair.

I'm intoxicated by streets safe enough for
mini skirts and late night sugar shining
from a Cadbury machine.

I can edit out the tests
I flunked, the chronic drizzle,
and that I was only popular

the night I dumped the coke
and everyone sought me out
to snort lint off my skirt.

Her Majesty's Pleasure

I'm not allowed to pee
until they peer up my crotch and ass, pretending

to look for drugs.
The floor has patterns on it, clumps

of grayish-purple circles that extend
from my feet to under the desk. I stare

at a crumpled candy
wrapper, the silver skulls

on my boots. Looking up
would make this real.

A foreign country isn't
a detective story. No one reads me

rights or offers a lawyer. Mostly
there's triplicate paperwork and waiting

for people on break.
The captain smokes

under a "No Smoking" sign
and is friendlier

to the hooker he's booking
than to the clerk

he send scurrying for a lost form.
Out of reflex, I smile

for my mug shot. They take my
ugly profile, of course.

My hands cooperate without
me, reach forward

to be grabbed and ground
into the pad. I'm surprised

by how much ink they need.
How it won't come off.

Ex-Boyfriend in Dresser

I find you in my top drawer,
naked and erect,
behind torn underwear and unpaired socks.

You handed me the camera
and grinned like a horse.
Keep you from bein' lonely, luv.

You are holding your love in your hand.
I might have laughed at you then; but I was trained
to be polite, and you were in a band.

Now you poke me with the memory of your bony
legs, prissy tailored suits and drunken lust,
your two swelled heads.

Broken

1.
I don't want to think
about broken things, the cracked
parts of myself I've covered, not with gold
resin like Japanese kintsugi, an amber river
meandering over the swell of a bowl;
but with yoga pants and sage smoke.
Each day sitting cross-legged to breathe into
believing that the past is gone and there is
only *now*. The clenched, clumsy
child really is gone. The teenager, terrified
in spikes and leather, gone. Red
streamers unfurling in syringes,
swept away. The AIDS-struck
boyfriend buried. Safer to think about
my air conditioner, humming
the way it's supposed to; though
three years ago the smug repair
guy said I would be lucky with another
season. Maybe some things can last
longer than expected, like the oil that sparked
the Hanukah tale my mother told
when she lit candles and prayed, then died
exactly when her doctors predicted.

2.
Though I can't sew, I long
to track down clothes
my mother bought me and
stitch them back – a patch over
the hole in the armpit, a new seam
in the crotch. How easily I once discarded
what was worn. The flowered

skirt with tulip buttons, gold-flecked
paisley jacket, countless pairs of jeans –
torn to rags or chucked into
the donation box. Like her letters,
heart-felt tomes I rushed through and
recycled, embarrassed, three thousand miles away,
eighteen and finally free. Her love
cloying, sticky. Not like the men
who would enter and leave me
back with myself, the drugs
which never lasted long enough. She was
always there – in my head, my
fear, my short legs. Fan
who treasured my terse
postcards. Background woman
I thought I could save for later.

Anchored to that Morning

Because you could not stop
the wind that tipped the boat, because

at eight you lacked strength to swim
into the lake's center where

your father thrashed, because you could do nothing
except scream into the useless air,

you want us to be lovers.
You are anchored to that morning, the sun

an unblinking yellow eye
over the water, your father

trim and smiling in a striped shirt, waving
as the boat pulls out.

When my sleeve shifts, exposing a map
of tracks, you grab my purse and block

the door, vowing to stay
in a sleeping bag on the floor. You distract me

with knock-knock jokes, pour baths,
and dole out methadone's bitter relief.

There was a tumor thickening
in your father's lung.

Told by doctors he
would have six months

of hospitals and pain,
he allowed the drowning.

Because a screaming child controls
your heart, because it is yourself

you want to help, you break
your vow, grab onto me, inflict wet

kisses, unbutton your pants
and pull me under.

Blood Tie

One blood test and the future
collapses.
I feel fine (tired,
sure, what mother isn't?) but the
numbers tell a different story.

Blood remembers
everything – every song
teenage hips thrust to, every hunger,
every bent, shared spoon.

Once bodies were safe.
Pam and I knelt beside a twisted
oak. So innocent, we pricked our index
fingers with a pin, then pressed
the bloody tips together, kissed.
Sisters forever.

I swallow mounds
of vitamins, sneak
to a doctor three towns away.
Double bandage each cut.

The present
wobbles.
My sick blood's a secret
that distracts me as I chat with other
moms at pick-up, brush
my daughters' hair. Each untruth
a tiny knife.

Eating Worms

*Nobody loves me, everybody
hates me.* My daughter dangles
pasta and sings, flicks her fork so
the strands dance and sauce

spots the wall.
I bite back sharp words.
This is the year
I learned to say, *my mother's
death, my husband's heart attack.*

*Down goes the first one, down
goes the second one, oh how
they wiggle and squirm.*

Long, tall slimy ones, short fat juicy ones. . .
I won't be the one to stop her song.

Acceptable

1.
That's unacceptable, my father barks
when I mention my toddler's
biting. *Well, she's frustrated*

and can't. . . He cuts me off.
Unacceptable. Just
unacceptable. The drumbeat of his voice

pounds, biblical. I stammer,
but the books say. . . , flimsy,
groundless as a corsage.

Unacceptable to Dad
when I was growing up:
noise, mess, backtalk, any type of lettuce

besides iceberg, lateness,
long hair on male heads
or female armpits,

mentioning the doors
my brother kicked in,
Democrats, dog sweaters, "Women's Lib."

A compulsive volunteer, my mother
socialized with women whose jewels and
houses made her voice shake.

Their daughters smirked at my
nameless jeans, changed tables
when I sat down. Mom told me

to wear make-up, braid my hair. I brought her
prizes and report cards, laid them at her feet
the way my cat delivers headless birds.

2.
My junior high school list
of how to deal with boys:
Never mention test scores.

Don't correct them.
Curl and separate eyelashes.
Use small words.

You, my sister whispered,
can do better
when I brought my first love
home. Stiff in a cheap
new jacket, he hadn't read
Homer, got pronouns wrong.

I can't be in the Pretty Club
unless I cut my bracelets off,
my first grader announces, gesturing at

bands of braided thread her
favorite counselor tied around
her wrist at camp.

She's mesmerized by
the mirror, keeps
changing her clothes.

3.
Recall after recall, the problem
isn't that there's lead
in children's toys, cups, jewelry,

toothpaste, wax vampire fangs, and vitamins,
but rather that the amount of lead
exceeds what the U.S. government considers acceptable.

My younger daughter and I
make a list
of things to do with Mad:

tell someone about it,
draw a picture, bite
an apple, squeeze a doll.

Where her sharp teeth clamped,
my forearm reddens and swells,
infection spreading.

For Any Occasion

To save my father
the bother of washing dishes
while she is dying, my mother
insists on paper plates.
She keeps a stash in the basement – boxes
of bowls and plastic utensils, bought on sale
and ready for any occasion.
Star-spangled cups call back
the July Fourth's of my childhood, picnicking
on a blanket, impatient for the sky
to break into light.
Vampires and bats in top hats dance
on napkins; a black cat perches on a pumpkin
carved by ghosts. Mom gave out candy
wearing wax fangs and a crimson
wig, turned my ponytails into ears
the year I was a dog, sewed dragon scales
across my brother's back. The bike-riding tiger
plate delights my daughter, and the crocodile
munching cake. Only Mom gets china,
for the broth she's allowed
after Dad clamps the bag
draining her stomach. As her hand shakes,
the tea cup clanks
against its saucer. My daughter
grabs the zebra from my hand.
That one's mine. I am left
with April Fools' Day bowls
or mud-brown plates
emblazoned with *Congratulations.*

III.

Another Word Not to Use in a Poem

"Buts" are always ugly.

Laure-Anne Bosselaar

Hidden in a butterfly
or butter, yes.
Just not the pale and flabby
conjunction, which needs

to lean against its
muscular cousins. Cigarette butts
are different. They add a sense of roughness
and often come with lyrical lipstick

smears or a cracked ashtray. Even better
are the butts of guns, which advance
the narrative. Human rears
as well are welcome, provided

one avoids the ugly
b-word. *Cabooses* are playful, *rumps,*
funny. Like most French things,
derrières hint at sex, and what

poem wouldn't be improved
with sex? Even lack of sex, the hunger
stirred by a curvy posterior,
imbues verse with bathos

and longing. Choose *cheek*
for a sensual specific,
while *ass* shows off
the speaker's passion or rage.

But

I break this rule in praise
of my tan husband's butt
as he steps from the shower,
flings off his towel and turns.

Stripper Rules

Imagine the man has a twelve inch penis
and avoid this area.
You can touch his shoulders

but keep your breasts out of his face.
Pubic hair is prohibited.
Showing tongue violates the law;

you can, however, open your mouth
and blow softly. There are three popular looks –
innocent, slutty, or sophisticated.

Make-up and gestures should match. Heels
must be at least three inches, unless you are in costume.
Then you can wear moccasins or boots.

Try related language.
As Pocahontas, say *How*.
Thursday is the best night,

then Wednesday, then Tuesday.
If you lack implants, highlight the butt.
Men are forbidden

to touch you. If a man does touch you,
take his wrists and push them down to his sides.
Try to make this seductive.

Find a way to hide
disgust or fear, perhaps by closing the eyes.
Do not tell him you're allergic to cigars.

Twat Ghazal

Lover, tell me what you see down there.
    I tried to look; it's hairy down there.
Jewel of many names – *lotus garden,*
    nappy dugout, muff, yoni, down there.
Long legs, slim hips, but Barbie's missing
    something – just a plastic V down there.
Men's nightmares feature teeth and razor
    blades – a cache of weaponry down there.
Thick books help frustrated women teach
    their men to solve the mystery down there.
If a date cooks dinner, he'll expect
    to dive into the sweet deep sea down there.
Slick magazines are full of vulvas
    and advice: *Don't smell fishy down there,*
Be creative – shave initials
    or a heart. Spread warm honey down there.
Kick him to the curb if he forgets
    your birthday or is lazy down there.
Science says men aren't creeps; nature makes
    them seek variety down there.
Forget my washboard abs and MENSA
    mind. You'll find the best of me down there.
You'll be my true love when you say,
    Alison, I'll spend eternity down there.

Pleather

He took her everywhere –
on pillows, pebbles, sand, the mossy

floors of forests. A boat's bathroom
at his niece's floating Sweet Sixteen.

He took her standing, kneeling, bent over Formica,
rolling on linoleum, scattering his

Fur is Murder pamphlets. Crouched
in a closed diner – neon

streaked their bodies as
they stuck to the naugahyde booth.

He took her slowly, tender explorations with lips,
tongue, each lingering finger. He took her quickly,

still half-dressed. And with costumes, feathers,
straps around her wrists, the whip's flick,

pleather only. *Yes oh yes* she murmured
at his prattle about the emotional lives of cows.

She grabbed burgers on the sly, stashed
mints near the lube.

He took her mornings before work, coffee breaks
when they could slip away. Always

before dinner. Often before bed. He took,
she gave, becoming bony and pale. Small

price to pay for pleasure, for desire lifting her
out of her ordinary life. Small concessions

to be sleep-hungry and less
available to friends, to hide her taste for meat, for blood.

Backyard Pond

After we killed the koi,
I swore off pricey fish,
opting for the ten-cent "feeders"
crammed in a back tank, marked
to be a snapping turtle's dinner.

You splurge on two big shebunkins,
which promptly disappear
to the muddy bottom.
You're building a rock wall, but
too late. Dirt has already tumbled
in, the water turbid as marriage.

Pulling weeds, we circle
each other, relieved to have a project.
When we sprinkle food, the feeders surface,
tiny but growing – Golda's burst of orange,
black-finned Jonathan and Jason, named for children
we won't have, silver Dharma
for the yoga teacher of our courting days.
Dharma has doubled.
Soon he'll be the size of the expensive ones.

Then, one by one, three ten-centers
float to the top; together we mutter
a prayer and bury them under weeds.
Golda, the only feeder left,
has a growth on her side.

Weeks go by.
She is still there! you show me, orange
flash that we have come to count on
while the large ones hide.
Every day we squat and search the murk
for that small, reliable flame.

Hunger

They have to wait to bury my mother
until my daughter stops nursing.
She had slept in a padded basket

while I stood wooden between my husband and my father;
people droned my mother's praises
and the coffin loomed.

Now she wakes and roots, all
hunger. A stranger takes us
to the rabbi's study. Amid clutter

of paper and books, I lift my black shirt. Broken,
numb, I cannot imagine my body
will respond, but her latch draws milk down.

She sucks dreamily. New to this world,
she knows nothing but a mother
who drips tears on her still-closing skull.

Her eyes flicker open and shut. Someone knocks,
asks me to hurry. I rub my daughter's back.
Her eyes stay closed now

but the fierce gums clamp.
I wait. The knot in my throat starts to soften.
As long as she holds on, nothing is

final. The drive to the grave
postponed, my mother is still above ground, here
with her new grandchild and me.

Photograph Found on a Table

Child
caged in crinoline, what do you see
as you stand wide-eyed with your family,
five women tense
in white dresses, the lone
man dapper in black? Who pushed your feet
into hard shoes? Tightened their bright
buckles? Whose hands snapped barrettes
into your wild hair? Silk snaked
around her throat, the bulky teen behind you
leans on a stark wall. You coil, set to
spring, as a stiff-wigged matron
(mother? grandmother?) vises one arm
and grips the other elbow. The man's thick fingers
press down on your shoulder.
You position one hand on each of their laps.
Ready
to push off. What do you see
and where would seeing lead
you, child, if you
let go?

The Diagram

Red's the color for longing,
with an arrow pointing
toward the one desired.

Sex is black with arrows
pointing both ways.
Most of the black's

just friendship fucking.
When we think there's love involved,
we put a red line as well.

Jenni puts red arrows toward all the boys
but Mark, who's been there longer
than us but hasn't moved up.

I love Paul, who's slept with
every guy and one exception:
a skinny, cat-eyed stripper. Almost all

the boys are bi. Jenni and I
are straight. Three weeks later
she'll decide she isn't.

Soon our slashes
overwhelm the page,
every third person joined by sex. We are

more connected than we'd believed,
bound with all the others
in a black and scarlet web.

Swimming with Frogs

Ripples connect us
in this bed of water.
Warm air thick from rain
obscures the stars.

Buoyed by darkness,
it is easier to speak
the shame our daylight faces
hide – prayer books

you burned, your mother's
madness; my scarred arms.
Each story a small
warty fist unfurling.

Chemistry

In a chemical change, chemicals change,
my eighth grade science teacher told us,

and to prove his point, a star rose
from the beaker.

Early morning, my body
plods on a treadmill, then sparks to a jog

at the sight of a bodybuilder
with the doe eyes of a

woman, yin and yang
in seamless balance.

Perfect men belong to actresses or
God, but the corner of my heart that denies limits

opens, just as in a crowd our ears perk to
the sound of our own name. As long as

I have eyes, I'll celebrate a man
who can transform me just by being

what he is. The treadmill's incline set on
high, I rise, my sex a smoldering star.

True, it's only chemistry, but angels
envy lust. Soon enough I will be

unaware of beauty as my bones burn
or my body sings itself to dust.

Who Would've Thought

The wind goosebumps our damp
skin as we lie entwined near the pond

listening to fish splash and the crickets'
din. After kids and cranky

sleep-deprived years, still the
dim, cloud-veiled stars dazzle. Dark

earth breathes beneath us as our
aging bodies wake and feed.

Intimacy

If you ask me again, I will tell you.
If you ask me with your sweet face
like a river, the words
will fly from my mouth.

Can you tolerate my fear of
the number six, of hospitals
and white horses, of babies
crawling endlessly across

my books? My fear that
I'll become a woman in an apron stirring
nails into soup? Deep inside me
is a cocktail waitress

and a married man with thick
fingers waiting to stroke her breast.
Remind me
the worm in my heart is a dream,

as in my dream the first woman I loved
tells my brother I look terrible and should
stay in the house. Remind me
in my waking life she bent

down in a park in Canada, handed me
a blade of grass, whispered
I wish you everything.
We are walking on yesterday's news:

*Beyond Baseball Cards – Stores Sell
Human Bones as Collectibles.* Three
skulls grin crookedly
beneath the headline. My longings

loop like ticker tape. Why tangle
yourself in my missteps and betrayals?
I can't even defend the edges
of my body. The man pressing

my thigh in the subway causes me
to shrink like a frog's muscle
hooked to wires in a lab. You tell me
you understand, that years ago in a barn

you unzipped yourself
into unbearable shame.
Every life has blood on its shirt.
Perhaps love is

finding a person to fill a hole
dug by somebody else.
Ask me again.

Author's Note

Alison Stone, *b. 1964*, is a poet, painter, Master yoga instructor and licensed psychotherapist with practices in NYC and Nyack. Her first collection, *They Sing at Midnight*, won the 2003 Many Mountains Moving Poetry Award. Stone is the recipient of *Poetry's* Frederick Bock Prize and *New York Quarterly's* Madeline Sadin Award. Her poems have appeared in over fifty journals and anthologies, including *Barrow Street, The Illinois Review, The Paris Review, Ploughshares, Poet Lore* and *Poetry*. The Stone Tarot deck (www.StoneTarot.com) reproduces Stone's 78 paintings of the tarot images. These paintings reflect integration and synthesis of art and mysticism. Currently, Stone and poet Kathi Aguero are editing an anthology on the Persephone/Demeter myth. She lives with her family in Nyack, NY.

Also available from Presa Press

John Amen
At the Threshold of Alchemy
Kirby Congdon
Selected Poems & Prose Poems
Kirby Congdon - 65 Years of Poetry
Hugh Fox
Blood Cocoon - Selected Poems of Connie Fox
Eric Greinke
For The Living Dead - New & Selected Poems
The Drunken Boat & Other Poems From The French
*   Of Arthur Rimbaud* (American versions)
Kerry Shawn Keys
The Burning Mirror
Transporting, A Cloak of Rhapsodies
Lyn Lifshin
In Mirrors
Gerald Locklin
Deep Meanings: Selected Poems 2008-2013
Peter Ludwin
Rumors of Fallible Gods
Glenna Luschei
Total Immersion
Witch Dance
Leaving It All Behind
Stanley Nelson
Limbos For Amplified Harpsichord
City Of The Sun
Steven Sher
Grazing On Stars - Selected Poems
t. kilgore splake
ghost dancer's dreams
splake fishing in america
Marine Robert Warden
Beyond The Straits
A.D. Winans
The Other Side of Broadway - Selected Poems

See www.presapress.com *for additional title information.*